SPRING VALLE

Pennie Stoyles and Peter Pentland

The A to Z of
Inventions
and Inventors

Volume 1: A to B

Smart Apple Media

This edition first published in 2006 in the United States of America by Smart Apple Media.

Smart Apple Media
2140 Howard Drive West
North Mankato
Minnesota 56003

First published in 2006 by
MACMILLAN EDUCATION AUSTRALIA PTY LTD
627 Chapel Street, South Yarra, Australia 3141

Visit our website at www.macmillan.com.au

Associated companies and representatives throughout the world.

Library of Congress Cataloging-in-Publication Data

Stoyles, Pennie.
   The A to Z of inventions and inventors / Pennie Stoyles and Peter Pentland.
   p. cm.
   Contents: v. 1 A to B – v. 2. C to F – v. 3. G to L – v. 4. M to P – v. 5. Q-S – v.6 T-Z.
   ISBN-13: 978-1-58340-804-9 (v. 1)
   ISBN-13: 978-1-58340-805-6 (v. 2)
   ISBN-13: 978-1-58340-788-2 (v. 3)
   ISBN-13: 978-1-58340-789-9 (v. 4)
   ISBN-13: 978-1-58340-790-5 (v. 5)
   ISBN-13: 978-1-58340-791-2 (v. 6)
   1. Inventions—History—20th century—Encyclopedias. 2. Inventors—Biography—Encyclopedias.
   I. Pentland, Peter. II. Title.
   T20.S76 2006
   608.03—dc22   2005057602

Edited by Sam Munday
Text and cover design by Ivan Finnegan, iF design
Page layout by Ivan Finnegan, iF design
Photo research by Legend Images
Illustrations by Alan Laver, Shelly Communications

Printed in USA

Acknowledgments
The author and the publisher are grateful to the following for permission to reproduce copyright material:

Front cover: photo of bicycle courtesy of Photoobjects, © 2005 JupiterImages Corporation

Photos courtesy of:
Australian Picture Library/Corbis, p. 6 (bottom); Australian Postal Corporation, reproduced with permission. The original work is held in the National Philatelic Collection, p. 17 (right); Corbis Digital Stock, pp. 30-31; Dreamstime, p. 26; Getty Images, p. 13 (right); E. O. Hoppe/Mansell/Time Life Pictures/Getty Images, p. 15; Library of Congress Prints & Photographs Division, p. 8; Clay Bryce/ Lochman Transparencies, p. 13 (center); Dennis Sarson/Lochman Transparencies, p. 13 (left); Photodisc, p. 14; Photolibrary/Martyn F. Chillmaid/Science Photo Library, p. 22; Photolibrary/Peter Arnold Images Inc, p. 12; Photolibrary/Photonica, pp. 6 (top), 24; Photolibrary/Science Photo Library, pp. 11 (bottom), 28 (top and bottom); Photolibrary/CNRI/Science Photo Library, pp. 10-11; Photolibrary/Cordelia Molloy/ Science Photo Library, p. 11 (top right); Photolibrary/Sinclair Stammers/Science Photo Library, p. 4; Photos.com, pp. 16-17, 20; Rob Cruse Photography, p. 18, 27, 31.

While every care has been taken to trace and acknowledge copyright, the publisher tenders their apologies for any accidental infringement where copyright has proved untraceable. Where the attempt has been unsuccessful, the publisher welcomes information that would redress the situation.

Inventions

Welcome to the exciting world of inventions.

The A to Z of Inventions and Inventors is about inventions that people use every day. Sometimes these inventions happen by accident. Sometimes they come from a moment of inspiration. Often they are developed from previous inventions. In some cases, inventors race against each other to invent a machine.

Volume 1: A to B inventions

Aerosol can
Airconditioner
Airplane
Antibiotics
Antivenoms
Aspirin
Baby car seat
Ballpoint pen
BAND-AID®
Battery
Bicycle
Bills
Braille
Breakfast cereal

They said it!

"Everything that can be invented has been invented."

Charles Duell, head of the US patent office, 1899

An aerosol can is a spray can. When you push the button on the can, the liquid inside comes out as a spray or foam.

Who invented the aerosol can?

A Norwegian, Erik Rotheim, invented the aerosol can in 1926.

The aerosol can story

Erik Rotheim was looking for a way to quickly apply an even coat of wax to his skis. He experimented in his workshop and eventually invented the aerosol can. In 1927 he decided to **patent** the invention. Another Norwegian called Alf Bjerke was the first person to sell aerosol cans in the 1930s.

By the 1940s and 1950s aerosol cans were very popular. They are now used for many products including deodorant, hairspray, paint, cooking oil, and even cream.

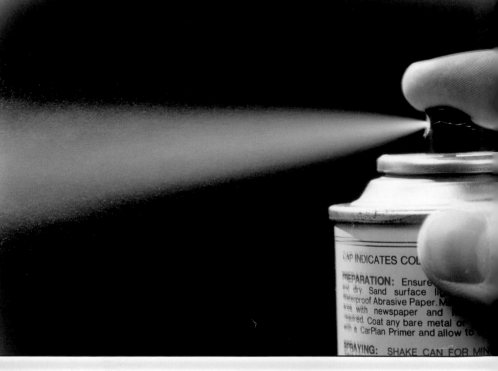

CAP INDICATES COL

PREPARATION: Ensure
and dry. Sand surface lig
Waterproof Abrasive Paper. M
area with newspaper and
required. Coat any bare metal o
with a CarPlan Primer and allow to

SPRAYING: SHAKE CAN FOR MIN

Did you know?

In 1998 the Norwegian government honoured Erik Rotheim by issuing a postage stamp with a spray can on it.

Pressing the button on top of the aerosol can makes the contents spray out.

How aerosol cans work

Aerosol cans work due to a substance called a "propellant." It is forced into the can under pressure and mixes with the other liquid, such as paint. When you push the button on the top of the can, the propellant rushes out through the dip tube, bringing fine drops of the other liquid with it.

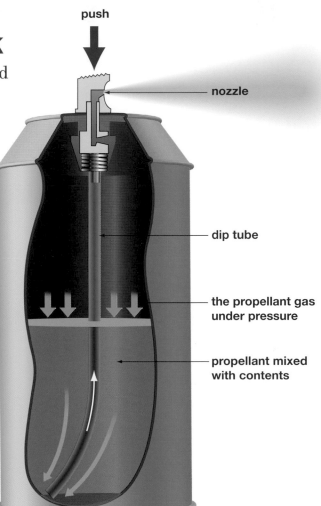

push

nozzle

dip tube

the propellant gas under pressure

propellant mixed with contents

Changes to aerosols over time

Up until the 1970s, a group of substances called chlorofluorocarbons (CFCs) were used as propellants. CFCs were harmful to the environment and they are now banned in most countries. Safer propellants are now used and pump spray packs that contain no propellants are becoming more popular.

Related invention

An Australian burns expert, Dr. Fiona Wood, invented an aerosol spray using a patient's own skin. This spray-on skin is used to treat people who have been very badly burned.

Glossary word

patent   a right granted to make, use, or sell something which is new, inventive, and useful

Airconditioner

Airconditioners are machines that make the air cooler. They lower the temperature of the air to keep people cool inside when it is hot outside.

Who invented the airconditioner?

American engineer Willis Carrier invented modern airconditioning in 1902. He invented it using a large refrigeration machine.

The airconditioner story

Willis Carrier's first job was with a printing company. When the temperature and **humidity** in the company's building changed, the size of the paper sheets changed slightly. This ruined the printing process. Carrier invented a machine to keep the building cool and to reduce the humidity of the air. He used a big refrigerator to **evaporate** water in pipes. Air from the building was cooled by being blown across the pipes.

Airconditioners are usually attached to a wall or window.

Willis Carrier (1876–1950)

Willis Carrier was born in Angola, New York. He graduated from Cornell University in 1901 and invented the airconditioner in 1902. By 1915 he had set up the Carrier Engineering Corporation which is still a world leader in making airconditioners.

How airconditioners work

In an airconditioner, a compressor squashes a gas and turns it into a hot liquid. The liquid travels around pipes and cools down. It then moves into other pipes where it evaporates, making the pipes very cold. Finally, a fan blows over the pipes, producing cold, dry air, which is blown into the room.

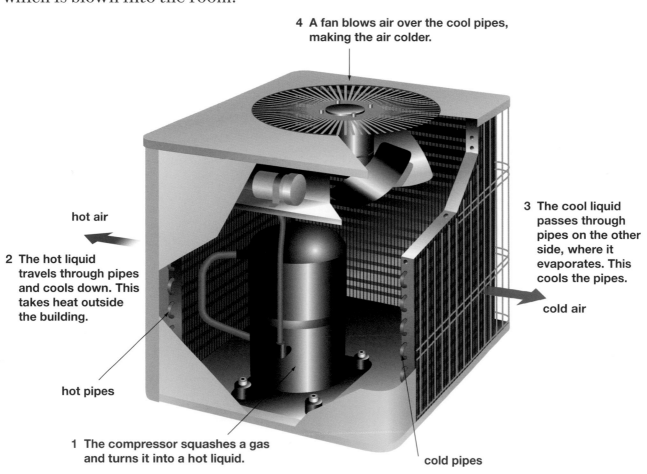

4 A fan blows air over the cool pipes, making the air colder.

3 The cool liquid passes through pipes on the other side, where it evaporates. This cools the pipes.

hot air

2 The hot liquid travels through pipes and cools down. This takes heat outside the building.

cold air

hot pipes

1 The compressor squashes a gas and turns it into a hot liquid.

cold pipes

Changes to airconditioners over time

Some airconditioners can work as coolers in summer and as heaters in winter. These are called reverse-cycle airconditioners.

Related invention

German Karl von Linde invented the modern refrigerator in 1871.

Airplane

An airplane is a flying machine that is heavier than air. It has wings and is pushed through the air by a motor or jet engine.

Who invented the airplane?

Many people contributed to the development of the modern airplane. American brothers Orville and Wilbur Wright made and flew the first airplane.

The airplane story

The Wright brothers were self-taught engineers who built printing presses and bicycles. They were inspired by the work of German engineer Otto Lilienthal. Lilienthal studied the flight of birds and used his observations to develop gliders.

The Wright brothers made the first powered flight of a heavier-than-air machine on December 17, 1903. The first flight lasted 12 seconds and covered a distance of 118 feet (36 m).

The Wright Brothers' first successful flight in an airplane.

Flight timeline

1783	Late 1800s	1903	1941
The Montgolfier brothers made hot-air balloons that could carry people	Otto Lilienthal made over 2,000 flights in gliders	The Wright brothers made the first powered heavier-than-air flight	The first jet aircraft flew in England

How airplanes work

Airplanes have a motor and a propeller. The propeller provides the power to move the airplane through the air. Airplane wings are tilted so they push air down as they move through the air. This means that when the air hits the wing, it pushes the airplane upwards. The air passing around the curved surface of the wings also helps the airplane fly.

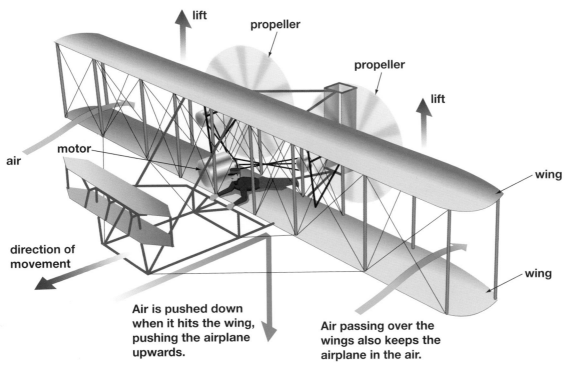

lift

propeller

propeller

lift

air

motor

wing

direction of movement

Air is pushed down when it hits the wing, pushing the airplane upwards.

Air passing over the wings also keeps the airplane in the air.

wing

Changes to airplanes over time

The American space agency NASA is developing personal airplanes. These vehicles will be kept in your garage and will be cheaper and easier to fly than private jets.

Related invention

In 1961, Australian engineer Dave Warren invented the Black Box Flight Recorder. It is used in every large commercial airplane to record cockpit voices and flight data. The black box is actually bright orange so it can be found easily if there is a crash.

Antibiotics

Antibiotics are substances that can kill **microscopic** organisms called bacteria. Antibiotics are used to treat infections and diseases caused by bacteria.

Who discovered antibiotics?

The first and most famous antibiotic, penicillin, was discovered by an English scientist, Alexander Fleming, in 1928.

The antibiotics story

Alexander Fleming was growing bacteria so he could study it. While he was on holiday, one of his experiments became moldy. When he got back he noticed that a mold called "penicillium" was killing the bacteria.

About 10 years later, a team of scientists, including Australian Howard Florey and German Ernst Chain, proved that the mold could cure serious infections caused by bacteria.

paper soaked in penicillin

bacteria

This dish has antibiotics and bacteria growing on it.

Antibiotics timeline

1928	1940	1943	1945
Fleming discovered penicillin	Florey and his team successfully tested penicillin on infected mice	Mass production of penicillin began	Fleming, Florey, and Chain received the Nobel Prize

How antibiotics work

Taking antibiotics stops bacteria from growing and multiplying by destroying them. Cuts can become infected if bacteria, which are all around us, get into the wound and start to grow and multiply. Your body can fight off bacteria, but if there are too many, you can get very ill.

Antibiotics are given by injection, as tablets, or in ointments.

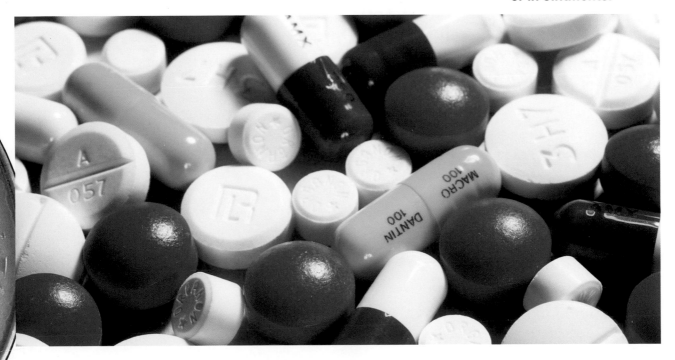

Changes to antibiotics over time

Bacteria can develop **resistance** to antibiotics. When this happens, the antibiotic can no longer kill the bacteria. One type of bacteria, called golden staph, is now resistant to all known antibiotics. Scientists are working to find a new antibiotic that will kill golden staph.

Howard Florey received the Nobel Prize for his work on antibiotics.

Related invention

The hypodermic needle, which can be used to give you antibiotics, was invented in the mid-1800s.

Glossary words

microscopic so small that you need a microscope to see it
resistance not being affected by something

Antivenoms

Antivenoms are used to fight off venom from poisonous animals. Some animals produce poisonous venom to paralyze or kill their prey.

Who invented antivenoms?

An American, Henry Sewell, made the first antivenom in the 1880s. A Frenchman, Albert Calmette, made the first antivenom that was used successfully on humans in the 1890s.

The antivenoms story

In the 1880s, Henry Sewell injected pigeons with small doses of rattlesnake venom, gradually increasing the size of the dose. The pigeons did not die because they had produced something in their blood to make them resistant to rattlesnake venom. It was called antivenom.

Albert Calmette performed similar experiments with horses and extracted the antivenom from their blood. His antivenom was successfully used on humans for the first time in the mid-1890s.

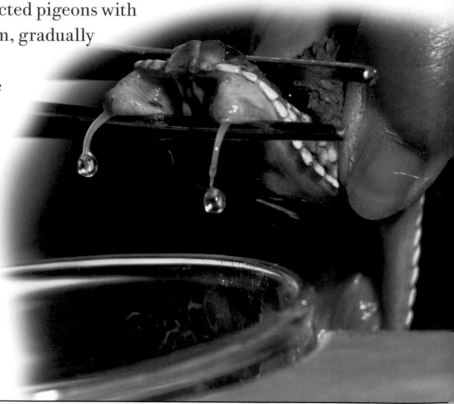

Venom from this snake will be used to make antivenom.

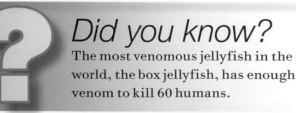

Did you know?

The most venomous jellyfish in the world, the box jellyfish, has enough venom to kill 60 humans.

How antivenoms work

Antivenoms act like glue. They stick to the venom in your blood and stop it from working. When your body cannot make enough antivenom to fight the venom, you need an injection of antivenom to help you.

Antivenoms only work against the type of venom they are made from. So if you are bitten, you should try to remember what the animal looked like. This will help the doctors when they are choosing which antivenom to give you.

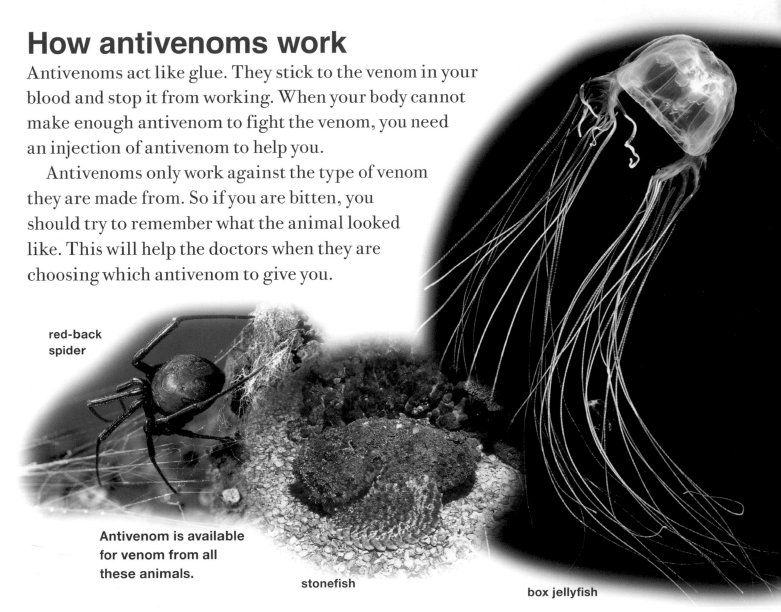

red-back spider

Antivenom is available for venom from all these animals.

stonefish

box jellyfish

Changes to antivenoms over time

Calmette believed that his cobra antivenom would work on all snake bites. He sent it to countries where there were lots of venomous snakes but he was soon proved wrong. Today, scientists are still trying to find one antivenom that works on many different types of animal venoms.

Related invention

Albert Calmette also invented a vaccine for the disease tuberculosis with Camille Guérin. It is called the Bacillus Calmette-Guérin (BCG) vaccine.

Aspirin

Aspirin is a type of medicine that is used to relieve pains, such as headaches and muscle aches.

Who invented aspirin?

The aspirin tablets we know today were invented by Felix Hoffman in Germany in 1897.

The aspirin story

In 1838, an ingredient in willow bark, called salicylic acid, was first used as a painkiller. It had an unfortunate side effect. It made the stomach bleed.

In 1853, a French scientist made a new version of salicylic acid called acetyl salicylic acid.

In 1897, a young German chemist, Felix Hoffman, was working for the Bayer company. He produced some acetyl salicylic acid and gave it to his father who suffered from severe arthritis. It relieved his pain and did not make his stomach bleed. This discovery was trademarked by the Bayer company and called "aspirin."

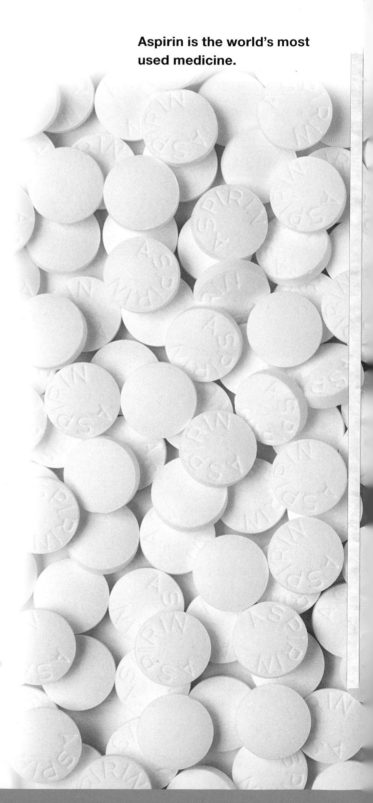

Aspirin is the world's most used medicine.

Did you know?

It is estimated that more than one trillion aspirin were taken worldwide in the 1900s.

How aspirin works

Aspirin works by stopping the body from feeling pain. Pain is caused partly by our nerves, but also by substances our bodies make. Aspirin works by stopping the body from making these substances.

Aspirin also makes your blood thinner so it takes longer to clot. Blood clots can block blood vessels and cause heart attacks. Many people who have already had one heart attack take some aspirin every day to thin their blood. This helps to prevent another attack.

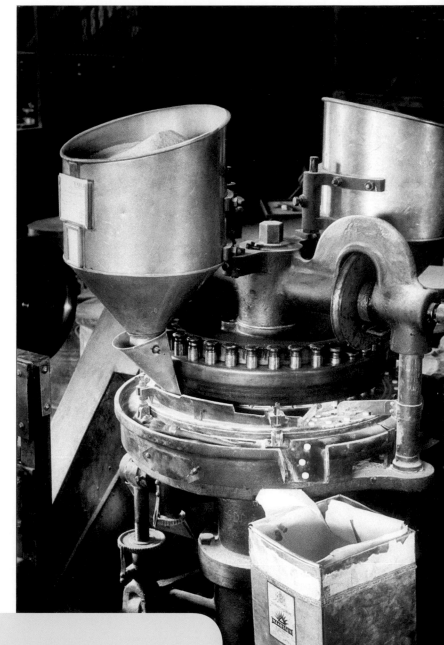

Manufacturing aspirin in the 1930s

Changes to aspirin over time

Taking too much aspirin can damage your stomach and your kidneys. Scientists are working to develop aspirin and other medicines that have fewer harmful side effects.

Related invention

Aspirin was the most popular painkiller in the world until the 1950s when paracetamol was invented. Paracetamol has an advantage over aspirin, because it does not irritate the stomach.

The baby car seat is a baby carrier that can be used to carry babies safely in cars. It is strapped onto the back seat with the seatbelt.

Who invented the baby car seat?

In 1984 an Australian company, called Rainsfords, invented the first baby car seat.

The baby car seat story

In the 1970s, Australia was the first country in the world to make seatbelts compulsory in cars. However, seatbelts could not protect babies. In 1984, Rainsfords solved this problem by making a plastic **bassinette** for babies that was encased in a solid frame. The frame, the bassinette, and the baby were all held in place by a seatbelt.

This baby will have a safe journey.

Did you know?

The first baby carriers for cars were invented in 1921. The baby was put inside a sack with a drawstring attaching it to the back seat!

How baby car seats work

During a car accident, a lot of force is generated by the collision. The baby car seat holds the baby in place so it cannot be thrown from the seat and injured or even killed. The car seat itself will move, so that the force of the collision is spread out and will not harm the baby.

This Australian stamp celebrates the invention of the baby car seat.

Changes to baby car seats over time

There have been many different baby car seats developed since 1984. Some can be converted into a car seat when the baby has grown.

Most countries now require babies to be carried in a baby car seat when traveling in a car.

Related invention

In 2003, NASA invented a child sensor for baby car seats. If a child is left in the car after the keys are taken out, the sensor sends a signal to a receiver on a key ring, and an alarm sounds.

Glossary word

bassinette   a basket in which a baby sleeps

Ballpoint pen

The ballpoint pen has a tube of quick-drying, long-lasting ink. The ink is released onto the page by a rolling ball.

Who invented the ballpoint pen?

Hungarian brothers, Laszlo and Georg Biro, invented the first non-leaking ballpoint pen in 1935.

The ballpoint pen story

Laszlo Biro was interested in finding ways to use the ink used to print magazines. He thought of using the ink in a new kind of pen. His pen used a rolling ball instead of a nib to write on paper. Georg Biro had the idea of connecting the ball to the ink supply using a tiny tube. The brothers developed their ideas and made the first pens for sale in 1944.

Ballpoint pens come in many different colors.

Did you know?

John Loud, an American, invented a ballpoint marker in 1888. He used it to mark leather. It was no good for writing on paper as it was too leaky.

How ballpoint pens work

The ballpoint pen has a ball that sits inside a tight fitting socket at the tip of the pen. The ball stops air from reaching the fast-drying ink inside the tube. As the pen moves across the paper, the ball rolls and spreads ink on the surface.

Air cannot move upwards past the ball. The forces of gravity and air pressure at the top of the tube push the ink down onto the ball.

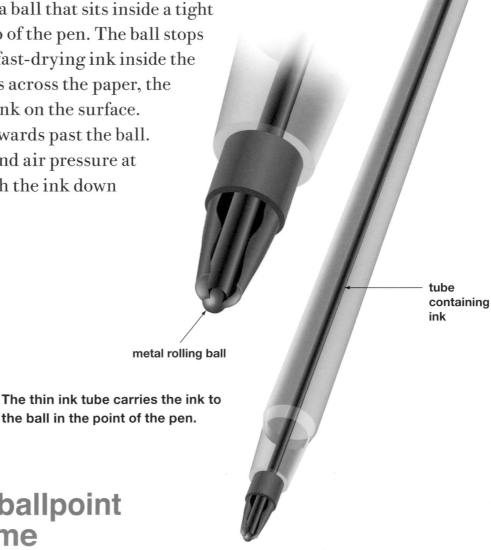

tube containing ink

metal rolling ball

The thin ink tube carries the ink to the ball in the point of the pen.

Changes to ballpoint pens over time

Marcel Bich bought the patent for the ballpoint pen and started making ballpoint pens in 1950. His BIC company sells 20 million pens throughout the world every day.

Related invention

Yukio Horie of Japan invented the first practical fiber-tip pen in 1962. The fiber-tip pen uses dye as a writing fluid, so it can be made in a large variety of colors.

BAND-AID®

A BAND-AID® is a type of adhesive bandage strip with a cotton gauze section in the middle.

Who invented the BAND-AID®?

American Earle Dickson invented adhesive bandage strips in 1920. He worked for a company called Johnson & Johnson, who manufactured surgical dressings.

The BAND-AID® story

Earle Dickson's wife Josephine was rather clumsy and often cut her fingers. Earle would put some cotton gauze on the wound and then hold it in place with a sticky cloth bandage.

Earle decided to put some cotton squares at regular intervals along a strip of sticky cloth bandage. Josephine was then able to cut off strips when she needed them. Earle told his boss about his idea and soon the bandages were being made with the brand name BAND-AID®.

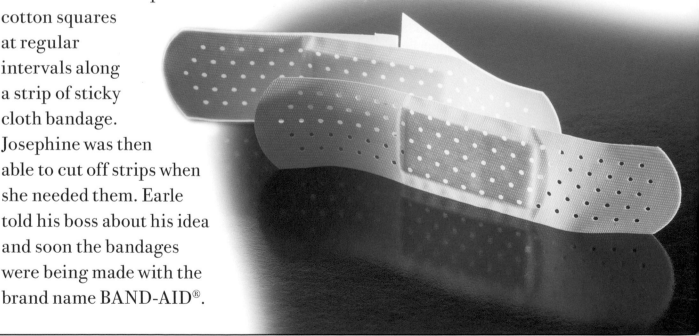

A BAND-AID® has a cotton square in the middle, and air holes all over it.

Did you know?

Cooks in food industries use blue BAND-AID®s. If they fall into food they are easy to see and remove.

How BAND-AID®s work

BAND-AID®s stop dirt, water, and germs from entering the wound and causing infections. This helps your body to heal cuts and scrapes. They also cushion the wound to help your body repair the damage caused by the injury.

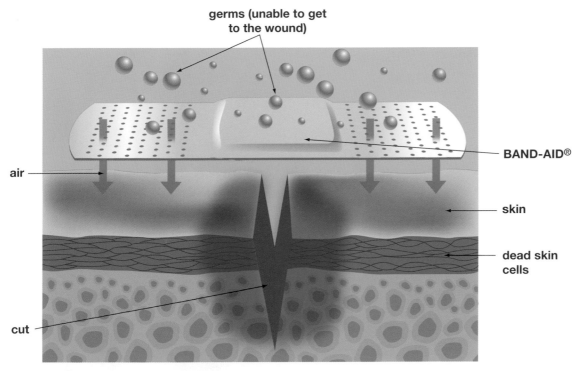

A BAND-AID® protects and helps to heal wounds.

Changes to BAND-AID®s over time

BAND-AID®s now come in a range of sizes and shapes. They are made of plastic and have air holes. These allow oxygen to reach the wound which helps the healing process. Liquid BAND-AID®s can form a seal over the wound without the need for plastic.

Related invention

Spray-on bandages might soon replace adhesive bandages. The spray was invented in 2002. It makes a fine web of fibers that block the wound and give a structure that new skin cells can grow on.

Battery

A battery is a portable and easy way of providing energy for electrical items. They come in many shapes and sizes, depending on the tasks they are needed for.

Who invented the battery?

Italian scientist, Alessandro Volta, invented the first workable battery in 1800.

The battery story

Twitching frogs' legs gave Volta the idea for the battery. In 1790, his friend Luigi Galvani noticed that a freshly cut frog's leg would twitch when it made contact with two different metals. Volta believed that this effect was due to electricity.

He discovered that when different kinds of metal were put in salty water they produced electricity. The first battery he made was a stack of metal discs separated by pieces of cardboard soaked with salty water.

Batteries come in many sizes, depending on the job they have to do.

Battery timeline

1800	1859	1881	1889	1954
Volta invented the first battery	The lead-acid battery that is used in cars was developed	The type of battery that powers today's torches and radios was invented	Rechargeable batteries were invented	Solar cells were invented

How batteries work

Batteries convert chemical energy into electricity. A regular torch battery has two **electrodes** that are separated by a thick black chemical paste. One electrode is the body of the battery, which is a zinc cup. The other electrode is a carbon rod in the middle of the battery. When you turn on a torch, the reaction between the paste and the zinc cup creates electricity. Electricity flows from one electrode through the light bulb and into the other electrode.

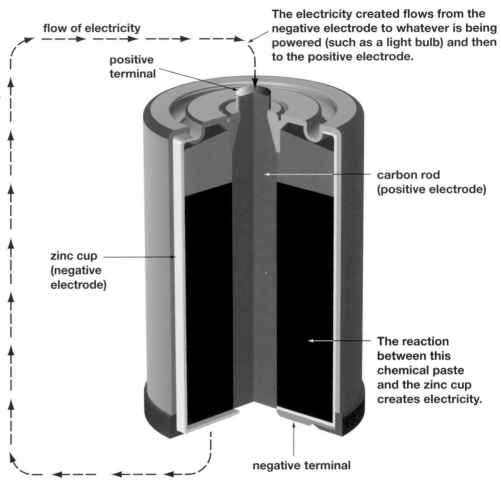

flow of electricity

The electricity created flows from the negative electrode to whatever is being powered (such as a light bulb) and then to the positive electrode.

positive terminal

carbon rod (positive electrode)

zinc cup (negative electrode)

The reaction between this chemical paste and the zinc cup creates electricity.

negative terminal

Changes to batteries over time

Batteries that can be recharged have been developed. This reduces the number of batteries being thrown away and harming the environment because of their chemical content. Some batteries use different chemicals and last longer than regular zinc-carbon batteries.

Related invention

Fuel cells are another way of converting chemical energy into electricity. William Grove invented the fuel cell in 1839. Fuel cells use oxygen and hydrogen to make electricity.

Glossary word

electrodes   parts of a battery where electricity comes out or goes in

The bicycle is an environmentally-friendly form of transport. It has two wheels, is lightweight, and is powered by the rider.

Who invented the bicycle?

The bicycle evolved for over one hundred years until it reached its current form. It was an Englishman, John Starley, who invented the modern form of the bicycle in 1884.

The bicycle story

In 1797 a Frenchman, Comte de Sivrac, invented the first bicycle, called the celeripede. It had two wheels, one in front of the other. Bicycles had no handlebars until 1817 and no pedals until 1858.

The term "bicycle" was first used in 1869. Three years later, the "penny-farthing" was made in Britain. It was called this because it looked like two British coins of the time, the penny and the farthing.

Englishman John Starley invented the "safety bicycle" in 1884. This was basically the same as the modern bicycle.

The "penny" was the large wheel and the "farthing" was the small wheel.

Did you know?

Fred Rompelberg of the Netherlands achieved the fastest speed on a bicycle in 1995. He reached a speed of 164.5 miles (268.9 km) per hour.

How bicycles work

The rider sits on the seat and pushes on the pedals to turn the front cogwheel. The chain running around both cogwheels then makes the rear cogwheel turn and the bicycle moves forwards.

Modern bicycle gears let the rider use more or less force when they pedal. Riders use different amounts of force depending on the type of surface they are riding on.

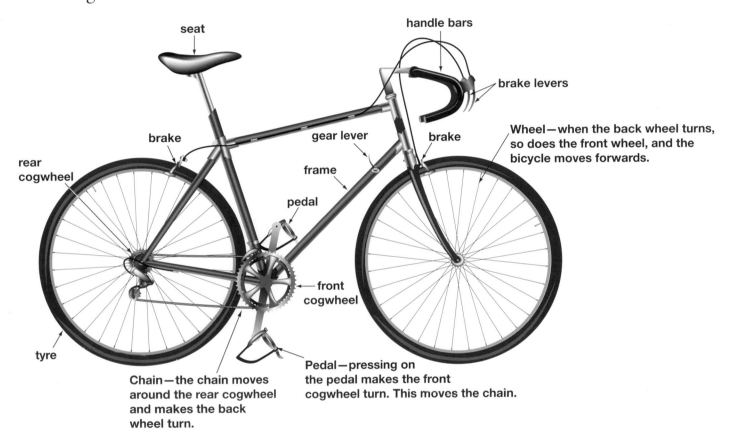

seat

handle bars

brake levers

brake

rear cogwheel

gear lever

brake

Wheel—when the back wheel turns, so does the front wheel, and the bicycle moves forwards.

frame

pedal

front cogwheel

tyre

Chain—the chain moves around the rear cogwheel and makes the back wheel turn.

Pedal—pressing on the pedal makes the front cogwheel turn. This moves the chain.

Changes to bicycles over time

There are now over 800 million bicycles in the world. That is double the number of cars in the world.

Related invention

The "recumbent" is a bicycle you ride lying down. It was invented in the 1930s by Frenchman Charles Mochet.

Bills are pieces of paper that have different monetary value. They are sometimes called "paper money."

Who invented bills?

The Chinese invented paper money in about 700, but the use of bills did not become popular until the 1700s.

The bills story

Before bills, people **bartered** for food and other goods. In some places, things like shells and cocoa beans were used as money. In the 1700s in Europe, people stored gold and other valuables with goldsmiths, who gave them a bill of receipt. People used these receipts as money. Banks copied this idea and began to issue bills that could be exchanged for silver or gold, and bills became a popular form of **currency**.

Different bills have
different monetary value.

Did you know?

In 1519, a Czechoslovakian count minted silver coins called *talergroschen*, which was shortened to taler. The word "dollar" is a variation of taler. The word "buck" comes from the North American settlers who traded in deer skins instead of money. A deerskin is also known as buckskin, which was shortened to "buck."

How bills work

Bills are printed by government printers on special long-wearing paper. Bills have many security features which make them almost impossible to **counterfeit**. Most bills have a security thread embedded in the paper. Bills also contain a watermark, which can only be seen when held up to the light. There is microprinting on most bills, which can only be seen with a magnifying glass. New bills also have color-shifting ink that changes color when viewed from different angles.

Microprinting is a security feature of banknotes.

Changes to bills over time

Plastic banknotes were invented by a team of scientists in Australia. The first plastic banknote was released in Australia in 1988. Plastic banknotes are now used in over 23 countries all over the world and this number will grow.

Related inventions

Credit cards are sometimes called "plastic money." In the U.S. in 1950, Frank McNamara issued the first credit cards. His cards could only be used to pay restaurant bills. Today credit cards can be used to pay for almost anything. One day, all bills may be replaced completely by credit cards.

Glossary word

bartered	to exchange goods and services for other goods and services
currency	any form of money
counterfeit	to make a fake copy

Braille

Braille is a system of printing for vision-impaired people. It uses raised dots that are identified by moving the fingers lightly over the page.

Who invented Braille?

Braille was invented by a Frenchman, Louis Braille, in 1824.

Louis Braille

The Braille story

Louis Braille was three years old when he damaged an eye with one of his father's tools. The eye became infected and the infection later spread to his other eye, leaving him blind.

When he was 10, he went to the National Institute for Blind Children in Paris. He learned to read there by feeling raised letters stamped on paper.

Later, he discovered an army system for sending telegraph messages at night that used raised dots on paper. He developed it into the system we now know as Braille.

A book written in Braille.

Did you know?

The first book written in Braille was published in 1829. It was called Method of Writing Words, Music and Plain Song by Means of Dots, for Use by the Blind and Arranged by Them.

How Braille works

Before Braille was invented, blind people could only read books where letters were raised higher than the rest of the page. They had to feel the letters and decide what they were. This was not easy to do because many letters felt the same.

The Braille system is easier to understand. Letters, words, and numbers are represented by a pattern of raised dots. Each Braille letter or number consists of up to six dots. It can be three dots high and two dots wide. This gives 63 possible combinations of dots. This allows the dots to also represent single words and punctuation marks.

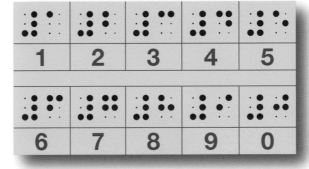

All the letters and numbers of the Braille alphabet.

Changes to Braille over time

Braille is now used all over the world in books for the blind. Most blind people can read Braille at about 200 words per minute.

Related invention

Raymond Kurzweil invented the flatbed computer scanner and software in 1974. It was part of a computerized machine that could read books and documents for the blind.

Breakfast cereal

Breakfast **cereal** is made from grains that are cooked and mixed with other things, including malt and sugar.

Who invented breakfast cereal?

James Jackson made the first breakfast cereal in 1863. It was the Kellogg brothers who made breakfast cereal popular in the early 1900s.

The breakfast cereal story

Up until the late 1800s, many people ate sausages, bacon, and other meats for breakfast. At the end of the 1800s, some people started believing that vegetarian diets were healthier.

In the United States, people went to health farms called sanatoriums, to learn about healthy eating.

One sanatorium was run by Doctor John Kellogg and his brother Will Keith Kellogg. In 1894 they accidentally made cereal flakes from wheat, which the people at the sanatorium enjoyed. Will started his own business and experimented with other grains. He invented corn flakes in 1906.

Cornflakes are made from corn.

Did you know?

Dr. James Jackson made bran nuggets that were so tough they had to be soaked overnight before they could be eaten. He called his cereal "Granula," but it did not catch on.

How breakfast cereals work

Breakfast cereals are made from grains. They are called processed foods because they go through several processes to turn them into breakfast cereal. To make cornflakes, each corn kernel has to be boiled, rolled flat, and then baked. Malt, a type of sugar, is also added.

There are many different breakfast cereals available today.

Changes to breakfast cereals over time

Many different types of breakfast cereals are available today. Many of the breakfast cereals that appeal to children contain a lot of sugar. Although breakfast cereals were invented as a health food, today some of them are very unhealthy.

Related invention

Swiss doctor, Maximilian Bircher-Benner, invented granola in 1900 in Zurich. His granola was different from the granola we can buy today. It was made with grated apple, lemon juice, milk, and nuts.

Index

Page references in bold indicate that there is a full entry for that invention.